THE
GREATEST
GOOD

For Belle and Melvin Lipsett,
who have taught me much about how
to do right in and by the world.

CHAR MILLER

PLATE 1

For George and Stellajoe Staebler,
who have shown me that the forest
is the source of many goods, including
beauty and artistic inspiration.

REBECCA STAEBLER

PLATE 2

THE GREATEST GOOD

100 Years of FORESTRY IN AMERICA

CHAR MILLER AND REBECCA STAEBLER

FOREWORD BY WILLIAM H. BANZHAF

INTRODUCTION BY JAMES E. COUFAL

Society of American Foresters

THE GREATEST GOOD: 100 YEARS OF FORESTRY IN AMERICA

Published by

The Society of American Foresters

5400 Grosvenor Lane

Bethesda, MD 20814-2198

www.safnet.org

Tel: (301) 897-8720

Fax: (301) 897-3690

ISBN 0-939970-80-5

Library of Congress Cataloging-in-Publication Data

Miller, Char, 1951–

The greatest good : 100 years of forestry in America / Char Miller and Rebecca Staebler.

p. cm.

ISBN 0-93997080-5

1. Forests and forestry—United States History. I. Staebler, Rebecca, 1957–   II. Title.

SD143.M495 1999

333.75'0973—dc21   99-41539

CIP

Printed in the United States of America

10   9   8   7   6   5   4   3   2   1

TABLE OF CONTENTS

PLATE 3

One faces the future with one's past.

PEARL S. BUCK, 1943

"The greatest good, for the greatest number, for the long run" was the ethic that Gifford Pinchot believed should define the mission of forestry. His words are just as relevant today as they were at the turn of the century. Contemporary foresters, like their predecessors, strive to meet the needs of the American people for a variety of products and services. At the same time, they are intent on enhancing forest ecosystem health, a necessity for ensuring forest goods for future generations.

We in SAF are proud to celebrate our centennial in 2000 through this review of twentieth-century forestry. We hope that *The Greatest Good* offers a visually stimulating way to better understand the profession and its many contributions to society. Although scientific knowledge cannot address all issues in contemporary forestry, we hope that this book helps enhance awareness of the need for science-based practices to meet many of the challenges we'll face as a profession, as a country, and as a world, in the twenty-first century.

To our readers in the forestry profession, we encourage you to use this book to remember or learn about practices that have worked, as well as those that have not. Such reevaluations will help us remain leading stewards of America's forests. Quite simply, our pride in the best of yesterday must always be placed behind our commitment to the best of tomorrow.

I would like to take this opportunity to thank Char Miller for sharing his extensive historical knowledge of the forestry profession and his assistance in placing events in a context that provides the perspective we need to more clearly see ourselves and our predecessors. To my associate, Rebecca Staebler, I would like to express my admiration for her ability to take the spark of an idea to what you see before you. Without her leadership and insistence on quality and balance, this project would not have been completed.

Finally, even though we have tried hard to make this book as comprehensive and inclusive as possible, given the availability of photographs and limitations of space we may not have covered all aspects of the broader history of American forestry; we apologize for any such gaps. For my fellow foresters and natural resource professionals, we hope you find something of yourselves in this history. For all other readers, we hope you gain a better understanding of forestry's past and your role as a partner in our future.

WILLIAM H. BANZHAF
Executive Vice-President
Society of American Foresters

PLATE 4

The forest is the most highly organized

portion of the vegetable world. It takes

its importance less from the individual

trees which help to form it than from the

qualities which belong to it as a whole.

GIFFORD PINCHOT, 1917

The very first image in this book of grand images shows sawyers sitting on a large stump in the Pacific Northwest. It is an arresting photograph, and one that captures the nineteenth century's emphasis on logging, and logging old-growth at that: Timber!

Early on, when forests were thought to be inexhaustible, forestry was associated with logging, perceived timber famines, and unmanaged cuttings. But the science of forestry went many steps further in the twentieth century, developing the notion that forests are not inexhaustible but renewable. Forestry is the only profession with the expertise, experience, and interest to manage forests for both present and future needs.

As the images in *The Greatest Good* attest, early foresters managed the land for water, fish and wildlife, recreation, aesthetics, and forage, as well as timber. They were also concerned with the health and management of trees in urban areas. To this day the profession struggles to determine the centrality of timber management in the scheme of multiple use. This is a daunting but necessary debate, since forests are a vital source and essential resource of life.

It is equally necessary to recognize, as this book does, that many of today's controversies are old packages wrapped in new paper. The proper balance between preservation and utilization, the role of fire in forest management, the use of pesticides, the search for a durable and effective land ethic, and the desire to ensure sustainable environments and economies have cycled through forest history like the lifecycles that define the forests themselves.

What can we learn from these cycles, and what might they mean for our future?

One possible answer is contained in Jane Difley's concluding metaphor. She suggests that we think of our movement toward the future as one of a stream that splinters and meanders, rather than as a fixed path. For me this implies that our future will be as our past, for we have, over the past one hundred years, been shaping and responding to the ever-changing physical, social, and political environment in which we work. Given the complexity and longevity of the ecosystems we manage, this is the only way it can be.

It is this kind of complexity that is reflected in *The Greatest Good*, a photographic history that paints a picture of a proud past, tells us something of how we got where we are, and gives strong hints as to the direction of those meandering and converging streams.

JAMES E. COUFAL
1999 President
Society of American Foresters

PLATE 5

CHAPTER ONE

PLATE 6

The groves were God's first temples. Ere man learned

To hew the shaft, and lay the architrave,

And spread the roof above them—ere he framed

The lofty vault, to gather and roll back

The sound of anthems; in the darkling wood,

Amidst the cool and silence, he knelt down,

And offered to the Mightiest solemn thanks

And supplication.

WILLIAM CULLEN BRYANT, 1824

PLATE 6
"In the Woods," 1855

ROOTS

William Cullen Bryant's lyrical description of the forest as "God's first temple," a cultural sensibility evoked as well in Asher Durand's painting, is reinforced through Tocqueville's assessment of the early nineteenth-century American temper: many citizens of the new nation believed their moral character and political destiny were inextricably linked to divine sanction and were made manifest in this most bountiful land. But the French aristocrat's perception also played out in the daily struggle of ordinary Americans to wrest food and shelter from this landscape of plenty.

Most plentiful were the vast forests that stretched from Maine to the Pacific Northwest. Although broken by prairies, grasslands, and mountains, they were so extensive that generations of Americans assumed they were endless. Out of these dense thickets, they carved agricultural holdings, framed houses, laid down corduroy roads, constructed canal locks, and burned cord after cord for heat and as fuel for engines, furnaces, and foundries. By midcentury, New England was deforested, a pattern that would be replicated as homesteaders pushed into the heavily wooded Great Lakes region and later penetrated the intermountain and coastal valleys of the Far West.

The celerity with which stands of chestnut, hemlock, tulip poplar, white pine, redwood, and fir were harvested undercut the perception of nature's limitless bounty and generated deep concern about the social and economic consequences of a treeless continent. One of those who put his worries down on paper was George Perkins Marsh; his *Man and Nature* (1864) became a classic articulation of humans' deleterious impact on the environment and a powerful assertion of their obligation to restore battered landscapes through conservative resource management.

Those who picked up on and then extended his ideas included some of the central players in the early conservation movement of the late nineteenth century: George Bird Grinnell, who helped found the Audubon Society and later the Boone and Crockett Club; John Muir, first president of the Sierra Club; Bernhard E. Fernow, who headed the federal Bureau of Forestry; and his energetic successor, Gifford Pinchot. Through private organizations and governmental agencies, together and separately, they labored to persuade their fellow citizens to enact legislation establishing forest preserves, regulate timber production, and alter patterns of wood consumption. The rewards, they argued, were worth the behavioral changes: the United States would enjoy a more durable prosperity while experiencing greater social mobility and a healthier environment—benefits that would help it meet the pressing challenges of the new century.

Among the lucky circumstances that favored the establishment and assured the maintenance of a democratic republic in the United States the most important was the choice of the land itself in which the Americans live. Their fathers gave them a love of equality and liberty but it was God who, by handing a limitless continent over to them, gave them the means of long remaining equal and free.

ALEXIS DE TOCQUEVILLE, 1835

PLATE 7
*Mature Douglas-fir trees,
Pacific Northwest, 1926*

Timeline

1785
Congress authorizes rectangular system for survey of public lands and authorizes land sales, while granting certain lands to states and reserving certain lands for public purposes

1812
General Land Office is established to oversee disposal of public lands

1817
Secretary of the Navy is authorized to reserve lands producing live oak and red cedar

1824
Bureau of Indian Affairs is created

1832
Arkansas Hot Springs is preserved from entry and private appropriation or acquisition

1835
Ralph Waldo Emerson writes the essay "Nature"

1845
Johnny Appleseed dies

1848
American Association for the Advancement of Science is organized

1849
US Department of the Interior is established

1854
Walden; Or, Life in the Woods, by Henry David Thoreau, is published

PLATE 8

PLATE 10

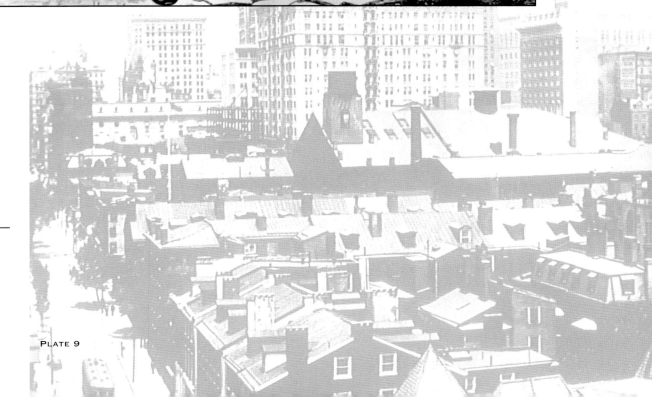

PLATE 9
Philadelphia, 1913

PLATE 10
Gathering fuelwood

PLATE 11
Maine woods scene

PLATE 9

We crossed one tract, on the bank of the river, of more than a hundred acres of heavy timber, which had just been felled and burnt over, and was still smoking....The trees lay at full length...all black as charcoal, but perfectly sound within, still good for fuel or timber....Here were thousands of cords, enough to keep the poor of Boston and New York amply warm for a winter.

HENRY DAVID THOREAU, 1848

PLATE 11

3

1862

US Department of Agriculture is established

1862

Homestead Act enables settlers to acquire 160 acres of public land after residing on it for five years

1864

George Perkins Marsh writes *Man and Nature, or Physical Geography as Modified by Human Action*

1864

Federal government grants California land for Yosemite Valley Park (returned to federal ownership in 1906)

1868–69

Gypsy moth is accidentally introduced in Medford, Massachusetts

PLATE 12

1870

American Fisheries Society is established

1871

1,280,000 acres burn and 1,500 die in the Peshtigo, Wisconsin, fire

1872

President Grant signs Yellowstone National Park bill

The National Arbor Day Foundation®

1872

Nebraska observes "Tree-Planting Day," which becomes national Arbor Day

1873

Timber Culture Act authorizes 160 acres of timberland for settlers, to stop theft, fraud, and abuse

AMERICAN FORESTS®
PEOPLE CARING FOR TREES AND FORESTS SINCE 1875

1875

American Forestry Association is organized; organization is renamed American Forests in 1992

PLATE 13

PLATE 14

Americans living in both the city and country have long depended on the forest to supply a rich array of goods. They used wood to build and fuel their homes and factories and entered the forest for everything from turpentine to tannin to maple syrup. Even fire, which often raged through homesteads and townships, did not deter people's desire to live in and with the forest.

PLATE 13
*Tapping maple syrup,
New York, 1904*

PLATE 14
*Fire in Peshtigo,
Wisconsin, 1871*

PLATE 15
*Stripping bark of tanoak
trees to produce tannin,
used in tanning leather,
northern California*

PLATE 15

1876
Franklin B. Hough is appointed first federal forestry agent

1876
Appalachian Mountain Club begins working to protect mountains and rivers

1876
Forestry science is prominently featured at Paris Universal Exposition

1878
Free Timber Act enables settlers in some western states to cut timber on public mineral lands without payment

1878
Timber and Stone Act authorizes sale of certain western timberlands, but weakens trespass and theft prosecution

PLATE 16

PLATE 17

PLATE 18

As timbering began to meet the needs of the broader population and support activities outside a local area, it required the work of men and machines. In the Adirondacks, the Southwest, the Pacific Northwest, and everywhere in between, wood was cut and transported by river and rail.

PLATE 17
Arizona Lumber and Timber Company, 1890

PLATE 18
Loggers, Washington State

PLATE 19
Loggers, Adirondacks, late 1880s

PLATE 19

PLATE 20

PLATE 21

PLATE 22

PLATE 20
*Apache Lumber
Company, Cooley,
Arizona, 1890*

PLATE 21
*Stewart River,
Yukon Territory*

PLATE 22
*Horse-drawn lumber
sleighs, Michigan, 1904*

PLATE 23
Port Blakely, Washington

A diverse resource, wood was essential for building and fueling various modes of transportation, from horse-drawn wagons and sleighs to trains and ships.

PLATE 23

1885
State of New York establishes the Adirondack and Catskill Forest Preserves

1886
Bernhard E. Fernow replaces Egleston as chief of the Division of Forestry

1886
George Bird Grinnell founds first Audubon Society

PLATE 24

1890
Yosemite National Park is established

1890–1902
Charles Sprague Sargent publishes *Silva of North America*

1891
Forest Reserve Act authorizes president to set aside forest reserves from public lands

1891
President Benjamin Harrison proclaims the Yellowstone Forest Reserve

1892
Sierra Club is founded by Joseph LeConte; John Muir is its first president

1892
President Harrison sets aside 13 million acres of forest reserves

1892
Timber and Stone Act of 1878 is extended to all western states

1892
Gifford Pinchot is hired as the first American professional forester on the Biltmore estate of George Vanderbilt in Asheville, North Carolina

"The President of the United States may…set apart and reserve, in any State or Territory having public land bearing forests, in any part of the public lands wholly or in part covered with timber or undergrowth, whether of commercial value or not, as public reservations…"

PLATE 25

Man has too long forgotten that the earth was given to him for usufruct alone, not for consumption, still less for profligate waste.

GEORGE PERKINS MARSH, 1864

PLATE 27

American conservationism drew heavily on the European experience: Romanticism flowed through Thoreau and Muir; Marsh wrote *Man and Nature* after seeing the devastated landscape of the Mediterranean; Grinnell embraced English hunting codes; and guided by Germany's Dietrich Brandis, Fernow and Pinchot introduced forestry to the United States.

PLATE 26

No woods, no game; no woods, no water; and no water, no fish.

GEORGE BIRD GRINNELL, 1882

Everybody needs beauty as well as bread, places to play in and pray in, where Nature may heal and cheer and give strength to body and soul alike.

JOHN MUIR, 1912

PLATE 25
George Perkins Marsh, c. 1820

PLATE 26
George Bird Grinnell

PLATE 27
John Muir, c. 1900

As head of the federal Division of Forestry, Bernhard E. Fernow recommended that *raupenleim*, or insect lime, a German preparation for the protection of trees, be used to control gypsy moth infestation in urban areas.

1896
National Academy of Sciences appoints special committee to investigate forest reserves

1897
Sundry Civil Appropriations Act (the Organic Act) identifies purposes for which forest reserves may be established, authorizes regulation of occupancy and use, and authorizes the sale of "dead, matured, or large growth of trees"

…I am getting more and more persuaded that what I learn here will be chiefly valuable as a sort of guide in the study of new conditions and the devising of new methods. Of course there is much that is general and true of both countries, but very much more that it would be foolish to attempt to transfer.

GIFFORD PINCHOT, 1890

PLATE 31

PLATE 32

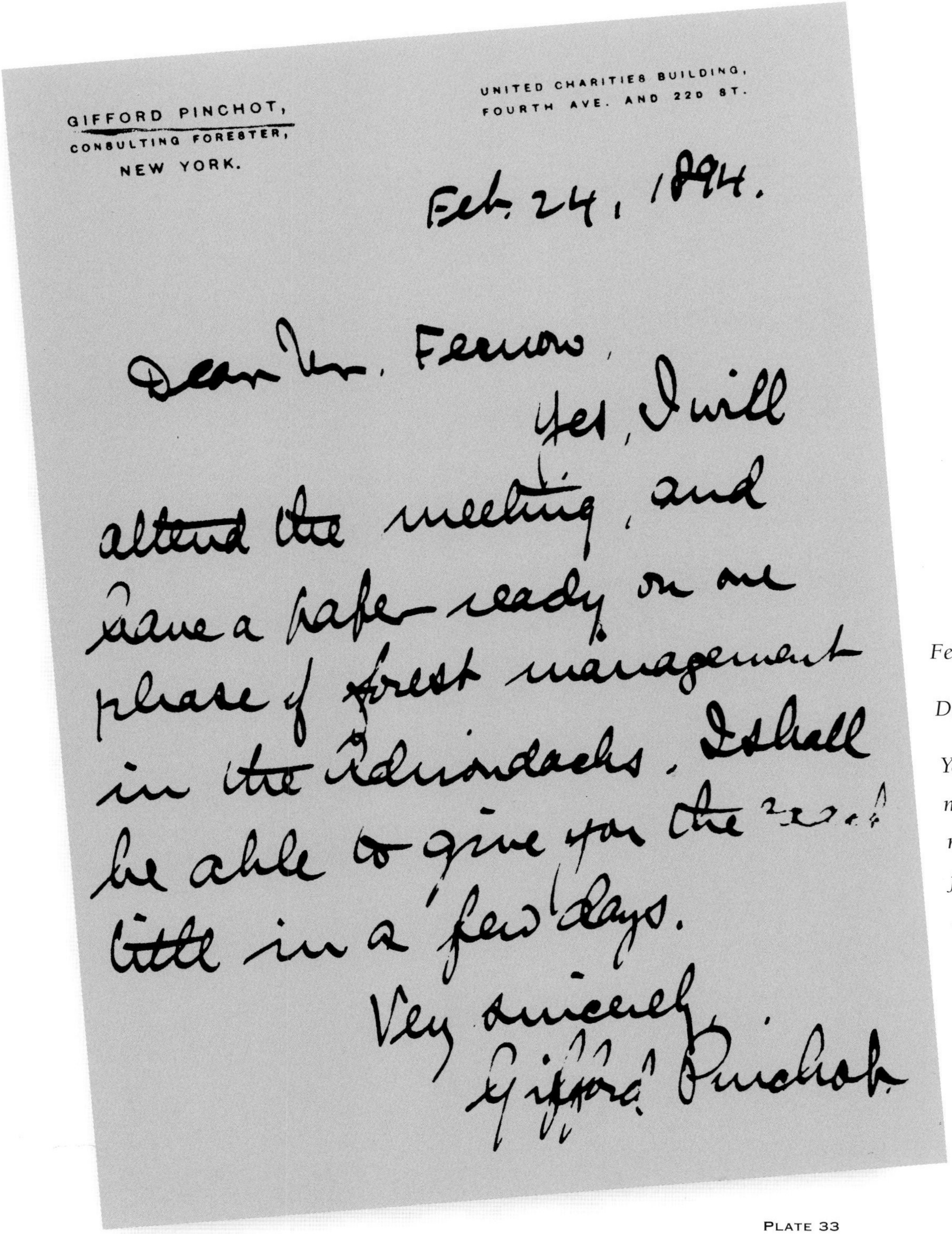

GIFFORD PINCHOT,
CONSULTING FORESTER,
NEW YORK.

UNITED CHARITIES BUILDING,
FOURTH AVE. AND 22D ST.

Feb. 24, 1894.

Dear Mr. Fernow,

Yes, I will attend the meeting, and have a paper ready on one phase of forest management in the Adirondacks. I shall be able to give you the exact title in a few days.

Very sincerely,
Gifford Pinchot

PLATE 33

Feb. 24, 1894

Dear Mr. Fernow,

Yes, I will attend the meeting, and have a paper ready on one phase of forest management in the Adirondacks. I shall be able to give you the exact title in a few days.

Very sincerely,
Gifford Pinchot

PLATE 31
Deitrich Brandis's excursion to German and Swiss forests, 1889

PLATE 32
Gifford Pinchot, Germany, 1889

PLATE 33
Letter from Gifford Pinchot to Bernhard Fernow, Feb. 24, 1894

CHAPTER TWO

PLATE 34

I believe that there is no body of men who have it in their power today to do a greater service to the country than those engaged in the scientific study of, and practical application of, approved methods of forestry for the preservation of the woods of the United States.

THEODORE ROOSEVELT, 1903

PLATE 34
Biltmore Forest School, Asheville, North Carolina, c. 1900; Carl Schenck stands third from left

EARLY GROWTH

President Roosevelt's confidence in the contributions foresters would make to the commonweal was not misplaced, just premature. The Society of American Foresters was only three years old, and the first schools—Biltmore (1898), Cornell (1898), and Yale (1900)—had barely opened (and Cornell in fact had closed, victim of an early protest over clearcutting in the school forest). Bernhard Fernow's editorial (at right), published in the first issue of *Forestry Quarterly*, reflects foresters' more cautious hopes for their profession.

Once the profession was established, foresters' knowledge would increase rapidly, a result of investment in education, the creation of the Forest Service—which hired many forestry graduates—and practical experience gained in public and private woods. The challenges these first professionals confronted, and worked to surmount, were many: fire and pest infestations led to scientific and technological breakthroughs; grazing on public lands required research on the impact of cattle and sheep; burned-over and heavily logged property forced public agencies and, in time, timber companies to initiate reforestation projects.

None of these developments were free of controversy. The introduction of steam-powered skidders, more efficient sawmills, and transconti-nental railroads intensified environmental despoliation and, as in the past, prompted demands for greater protection of the nation's forests. Public foresters were also under assault. During President Roosevelt's tenure, the acreage the Forest Service managed in the West multiplied quickly, an increase that was as hotly debated as the agency's decision to raise fees to control use. Political tensions were reflected in newspaper cartoons lambasting its chief, "Czar" Pinchot.

By the 1920s a more cooperative relationship between industrial and public foresters had emerged, especially for fire suppression. That decade also witnessed intensified recreational use of the national forests and designation of the first wilderness area. The trend toward tourism was reinforced during the Depression when on public lands the Civilian Conservation Corps built cabins, trails, and other amenities. In response to the growing demand for new housing, which like recreation would only accelerate after World War II, scientists developed more efficient uses of timber, such as plywood, and revolutionized the construction industry. The varied human benefits that now derived from their efforts gave professional foresters, as they headed off to war, the confidence that they had earned Theodore Roosevelt's early praise.

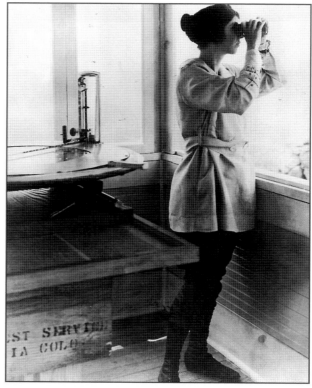

PLATE 35

Since no past masters of the art, but only a young generation of foresters, just beginning their work, are, for the time being, to be the contributors and editors....[the journal] must step forth with due modesty and with the expectation of deficiencies, which only experience...can correct.

BERNHARD E. FERNOW, 1902

PLATE 35
Helen Dowe, Devil's Head Lookout, Pike National Forest, Colorado, 1919

15

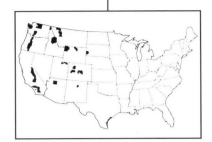

1898

Carl A. Schenck establishes the Biltmore Forest School in North Carolina

1898

Gifford Pinchot succeeds Fernow as chief of the Division of Forestry

1898

First four-year forestry curriculum is established at Cornell University in New York

1899

First timber sale takes place on a national forest reserve in the Black Hills, South Dakota

PLATE 36

PLATE 37

PLATE 37
Plant identification, Biltmore Forest School, Asheville, North Carolina, c. 1900

PLATE 39

PLATE 40

PLATE 38
Biltmore Estate, Asheville,
North Carolina

PLATE 39
Biltmore Forest School,
class of 1905

I had advised my graduates to seek employment with

the large landowners of timberlands rather than with

the Bureau of Forestry in Washington, because I

wanted them to be foresters in the woods rather than

foresters in office buildings.

CARL A. SCHENCK, 1955

PLATE 40
Students doing volume
table work, Biltmore
Forest School, 1910

PLATE 38

17

Timeline

1900
Society of American Foresters is organized, with Gifford Pinchot as first president

1900
Yale School of Forestry is founded with an endowment from the Pinchot family

1900
Frederick Weyerhaeuser founds the Weyerhaeuser Timber Company in Washington State

1901
Forestry Division is created in General Land Office to administer forest reserves

1902
National Lumber Manufacturers Association is formed

1902
First issue of *Forestry Quarterly*, predecessor to the *Journal of Forestry*, is published

1903
President Theodore Roosevelt creates first national wildlife refuge, on Pelican Island, Florida

Cornell University was the first collegiate-level institution in the United States to offer a four-year forestry degree. Bernhard Fernow was the forestry school's first director, and among its early students was William Greeley, who later became chief of the Forest Service.

PLATE 41

PLATE 41
l to r: Edward E. Carter, William B. Greeley, and Austin Cary

PLATE 42
Cornell forestry curriculum, 1900

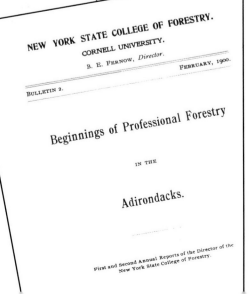

PLATE 42

NEW YORK STATE COLLEGE OF FORESTRY.
CORNELL UNIVERSITY.
B. E. FERNOW, *Director.*

BULLETIN 2.   FEBRUARY, 1900.

Beginnings of Professional Forestry

IN THE

Adirondacks.

First and Second Annual Reports of the Director of the New York State College of Forestry.

COURSES OF INSTRUCTION.

THE COURSE IN FORESTRY LEADING TO THE DEGREE OF BACHELOR OF THE SCIENCE OF FORESTRY.

The courses of the spring term in the junior and senior years will be given in the College Forest at Axton, N. Y. Students must therefore arrange their courses in other branches so as to keep the spring term entirely free for work in the woods.

[*Courses in parenthesis are elective in whole or in part.*]

Freshman Year.	No. Course.	1st Term.	2d Term.	3d Term.
Solid Geom. ⎫				
Adv. Algebra. ⎬ (Math.)	7	2	2	2
Pl. and Sph. Trig. ⎭				
Anal. Geom. ⎫ (Mathematics)	10	(3)	(3)	(3)
Calculus. ⎭				
Physics	2a	2	2	2
Physics	2b	(5)	(5)	(5)
Chemistry	1	3	3	3
Invertebrate Zoology	1, 3	3	—	3
Vertebrate Zoology	2	—	3	—
Botany	1, 2	3	3	3
Mineralogy (Geology)	10	—	3	—
Meteorology (Geology)	23	2	—	—
Forestry	1	—	—	2
Political Economy	34	—	—	3

Sophomore Year.	No. Course.	1st Term.	2d Term.	3d Term.
Chemistry	16	4	4	(4)
Entomology	7	—	2	—
Entomology	4, 5	(3)	—	(3)
Systematic Dendrology (Botany)	9	3	—	—
Biological Dendrology	—	—	—	3
Stratigraphic Geology	1	3	—	—
General Geology	21	3	3	3
Soils (Geology)	32	—	2	—
Pen Topog. (Engineering)	4	—	2	—
Land Surv. (Engineering)	5	—	—	4
Political Economy	51	—	3	3
Forestry	2	(3)	(3)	—

*All electives must be chosen at the beginning of the year with the previous

— 50 —

Junior Year.	No. Course.	1st Term.	2d Term.	3d Term.
Chemistry				
Botany				
Physical Geography (Geology)	21b	2	—	—
Systematic Zoology, Fish Culture and Game-keeping	22	3	3	3
Forestry		(3)	(3)	—
	19	3	3	3
	''	3	4	2
	13	4	—	2
	4	—	—	5
	6	—	—	5
	15	—	3	3
	12	3	—	5

Senior Year.	No. Course.	1st Term.	2d Term.	3d Term.
Political Economy	14	—	—	3
Law	59	(2)	(2)	—
Forestry				
	5	2	—	—
	16	4	—	2
	17	—	—	10
	9	—	2	5
	10	—	—	2
Seminary		3	3	3
		2	2	—

The courses in fundamental and supplementary branches are selected from those offered in the Departments of the University. Some of these courses are fuller than necessary for students in forestry, and may possibly be shortened, leaving more room for Electives. The courses advised are: Mathematics, 7; Physics, 2a; Chemistry, 1, 16; Zoology: Invertebrate, 1, Vertebrate, 2, Entomology, 3, 7; Botany, 1, 2, 5, 9, 11; Geology, 10, 21, 22, 23, 32; Engineering, 4, 5; Political Economy, 34, 51, 59.

COURSES IN FOREST

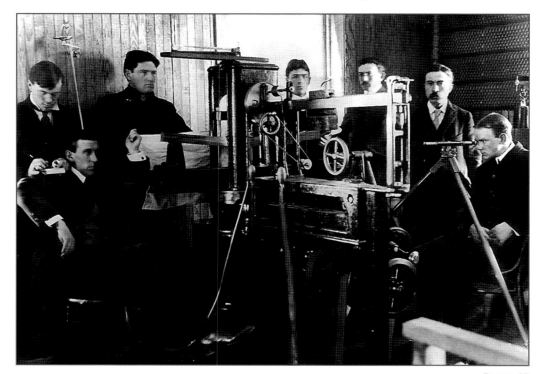

PLATE 43

The School of Forestry at Yale was founded with a grant from the Pinchot family in 1900. The first dean was Henry Graves (second from right, second row, plate 45), who later succeeded Gifford Pinchot as chief of the Forest Service.

PLATE 44

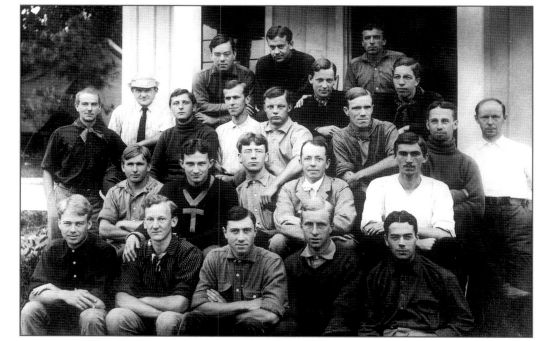

PLATE 45

PLATE 43
Marsh Hall, Yale, 1904

PLATE 44
Yale forest camp at Grey Towers, Milford, Pennsylvania, c. 1908

PLATE 45
Yale Forest School, 1906

| 1905 |
| National Audubon Society is organized |

| 1905 |
| USDA Forest Service and National Forest System are created by merging Interior's Forestry Division with USDA Bureau of Forestry |

| 1905 |
| Second American Forest Congress is held |

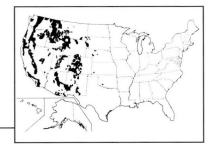

| 1906 |
| Forest Homestead Act opens agricultural lands for entry within national forests |

| 1907 |
| National forestland in the US encompasses 132.7 million acres |

| 1908 |
| White House conference of governors on conservation policy is held |

| 1908 |
| First forest experiment station is established at Fort Valley (now Coconino National Forest), Arizona |

PLATE 46

| 1908 |
| Congress directs Forest Service to share 25% of receipts with states for use on roads and schools in counties where national forests are located |

Western Forestry and Conservation Association

| 1908 |
| Western Forestry and Conservation Association is established |

This is the pen with which President Roosevelt signed the act of Feb 1, 1905, which created the Forest Service

Gifford Pinchot

PLATE 47

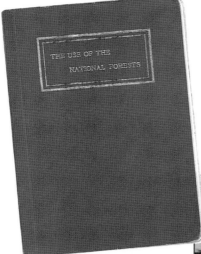

PLATE 48

National Forests exist today because the people want them. To make them accomplish the most good, the people themselves must make clear how they want them run.

GIFFORD PINCHOT, 1907

PLATE 47
Handwritten note by Gifford Pinchot

PLATE 48
1907 Forest Service "use book"

PLATE 49
Gifford Pinchot, Bureau of Forestry, c. 1900

PLATE 49

PLATE 50

It is not so much what a man knows when he enters the Service as what he is able to learn that counts. It would be impossible to cram the endless details of administration into the mind of the future employee by any process of schooling, for these things must be absorbed by doing them.

H.H. Chapman, 1918

Plate 50
Forest Ranger Griffen and Forest Guard Cameron, Lolo National Forest, Montana, 1909

Plate 51
San Isabel National Forest, Colorado, 1911

Plate 51

PLATE 53

PLATE 52

PLATE 52
Office of the supervisor, Leadville (now Pike and San Isabel) National Forest, Colorado, 1909

PLATE 53
Jim Sizer, Apache National Forest, Arizona, c. 1910

PLATE 54

PLATE 54
Sending messages using heliographs and the sun's rays, Washakie, Wyoming, 1918

PLATE 55
Forest Assistant W.H.B. Kent, Huachuca (now Coronado) National Forest, Arizona, 1905

PLATE 55

25

PLATE 56

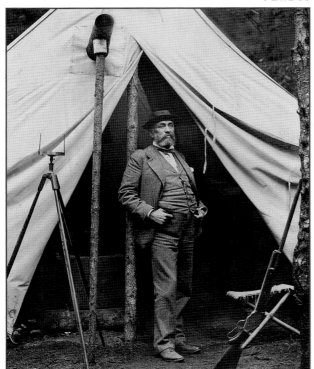

PLATE 57

PLATE 58

PLATE 56
*Forest entomologist,
California, 1903*

PLATE 57
*Colonel Fox, Hamilton
County, New York, 1900*

PLATE 58
*F.C. Craighead, W.D.
Edmonston, G. Hofer,
and F.P. Keen supervis-
ing control of bark
beetle outbreak,
Kaibab National
Forest, Arizona, 1924*

PLATE 59
*Forest Ranger Griffen
figuring distance to
smoke sighted, Cabinet
National Forest,
Montana, 1909*

PLATE 60
*Helen Dowe using
Osborne Fire Finder,
Devil's Head Lookout,
Colorado, 1919*

PLATE 59

PLATE 60

Weyerhauser Timber Co.
Camp #1 King Co. Wash.
SW¼ OF SE¼ Sec 2 T22 N R.7E
By L. HEATH, July. 1st 1903

PLATE 61

Private forestry was also developing in the early twentieth century.
Frederick Weyerhaeuser started the Weyerhaeuser Timber Company
in Washington State in 1900, hiring George S. Long as the company's first
timberlands manager. Long stands above on a skid road, made of short logs
laid crossways, which enabled loggers to transport logs out of the forest.

PLATE 61
*George S. Long, King
County, Washington,
1903*

PLATE 62
*The Vanzer homestead
in Washington, 1906*

The great, dark trees of the Big

Woods stood all around the house,

and beyond them were other trees

and beyond them were more trees. As

far as a man could go to the north in

a day, or a week, or a whole month,

there was nothing but woods.

LAURA INGALLS WILDER, 1932

PLATE 62

While young foresters were being educated and trained in universities, families from Texas to Washington continued to base their lives and livelihood in and around the forest— some quite literally!

PLATE 63

PLATE 63
Texas homestead

PLATE 64

PLATE 65

PLATE 66

PLATE 67

PLATE 68

PLATE 69

PLATE 70

PLATE 71

From survey to sawmill, from Arkansas to Washington and Michigan to Arizona, crews were at work in the woods, supported by cooks, saw sharpeners, and drivers. And when the work was done, the land cleared, and the logs transported by horse, train, or ship, the crews moved on to work in yet another vast and plentiful forest.

PLATE 68
Cypress timber, southern Arkansas

PLATE 69
Timber estimate note-book, Arizona Land and Timber Company, 1900

PLATE 70
George Banzhaf running lines for forest inventory, Michigan, 1922

PLATE 71
Preparing for uneven-aged timber sale, Wisconsin, 1927

PLATE 72

PLATE 73

PLATE 72
*Old-growth pine,
Thompson Lumber
Company, Texas, c. 1910*

PLATE 73
*Removing logs using log
skids, Little River Lumber
Company, Smoky
Mountains, Tennessee,
early 1920s*

PLATE 74
*Kenny logging camp,
south of Flagstaff,
Arizona, 1904*

PLATE 74

PLATE 75

PLATE 75
*Logging crew,
Thompson Lumber
Company, Texas,
c. 1908*

PLATE 76
*Salvaging cedar using
steam falling saw*

PLATE 77
*Crew with yarding
donkey*

PLATE 78
*Crew with big wheels,
10 feet high, used for
dragging logs*

PLATE 76

PLATE 77

PLATE 78

PLATE 79

Clemmons Log. Co.
C. K. Kinsey Photo
No. 483

The average woodchopper spends 35 minutes a day in food assimilation. [Yet] there is in each camp a fastest man or group of men who waste but 21 minutes diurnally in the mad dash for sustenance.

ROBERT MARSHALL, 1929

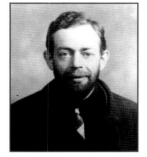

PLATE 80

PLATE 81

PLATE 83

PLATE 82

PLATE 79
Clemons Logging Company workers, Washington

PLATE 80
Robert Marshall

PLATE 81
Kitchen, Cherry Valley Logging Company, Washington

PLATE 82
Railroad car camp, Michigan

PLATE 83
Saw-sharpener's shop, Clemons Logging Company, Melbourne, Washington, c. 1920

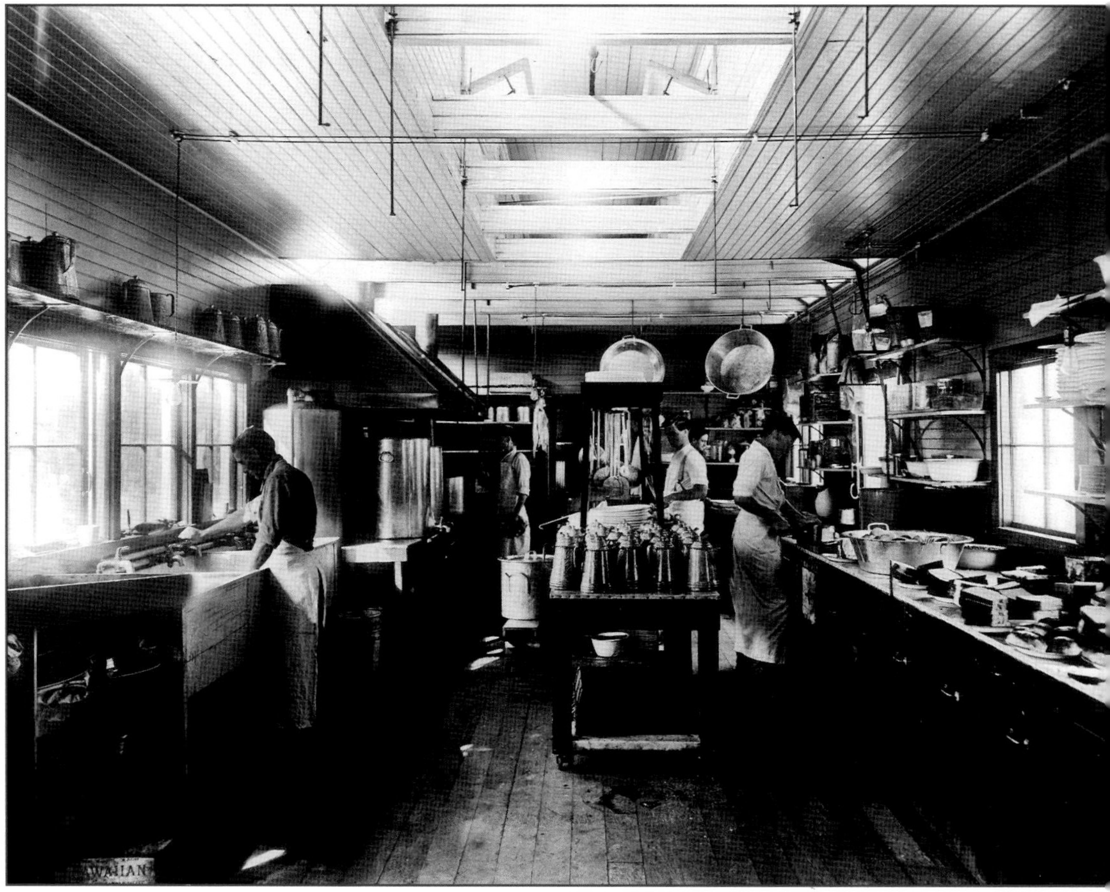

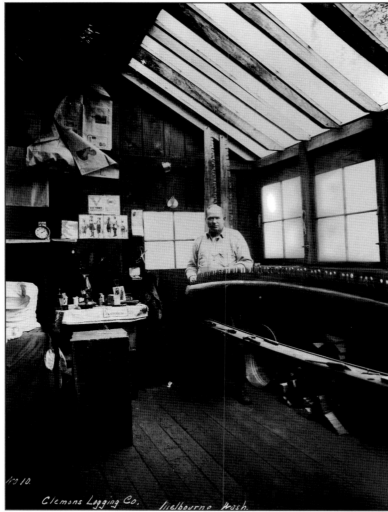

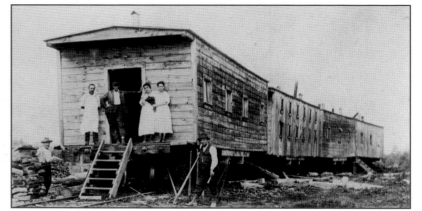

PLATE 84

PLATE 85

PLATE 86

PLATE 87

PLATE 84
Marquette Dead River sawmill, Presque Isle, Michigan

PLATE 85
Head saw and carriage with fir log, Snoqualmie Falls Lumber Company, Washington

PLATE 86
Log raft en route to mill, Washington, 1910

PLATE 87
Logging train on 100-foot railroad trestle, Pacific Northwest

PLATE 88
Land logged and cleared for farming in the early 1900s, Upper Peninsula, Michigan

PLATE 89
Moving day, Cherry Valley Logging Company, Washington

PLATE 88

PLATE 89

The American Colossus was fiercely intent on appropriating and exploiting the riches of the richest of all continents—grasping with both hands, reaping where he had not sown, wasting what he thought would last forever. New railroads were opening up new territory. The exploiters were pushing farther and farther into the wilderness. The man who could get his hands on the biggest slice of natural resources was the best citizen. Wealth and virtue were supposed to trot in double harness.

GIFFORD PINCHOT, 1947

1910

President Taft fires Gifford Pinchot over dispute with secretary of the Interior and names Henry S. Graves new chief of Forest Service

1910

Forest Products Laboratory is established in Madison, Wisconsin

PLATE 90

1910

Extensive fires burn in the northern Rockies, including more than 3 million acres in Idaho and Montana

1911

Weeks Law authorizes purchase of lands, including those east of the Great Plains, for national forests to protect navigable streams

PLATE 91

1911

Supreme Court holds that Congress can create national forests, that the secretary of Agriculture can issue regulations governing use, and that fees can be charged for such use

1913

William T. Hornaday, head of New York Zoological Society, writes *Our Vanishing Wildlife, Its Extermination and Preservation*

1913

Hetch Hetchy Dam in Yosemite National Park is approved by Congress

1913–14

Bureau of Corporations issues report on the lumber industry

1914

Southern Pine Association is established

1915

Ecological Society of America is formed

PLATE 92

PLATE 94

PLATE 93

PLATE 92
Effects of overgrazing, San Isabel National Forest, Colorado, 1912

PLATE 93
Political cartoon, c. 1908

PLATE 94
Counting sheep, Wasatch National Forest, Utah, 1914

PLATE 95
Rocky Mountain News, *September 20, 1908*

PLATE 96
Spokesman Review, *1908*

We have become great in a material sense because of the lavish use of our resources, and we have just reason to be proud of our growth. But the time has come to inquire seriously what will happen when our forests are gone.

THEODORE ROOSEVELT, 1908

PLATE 95

UNCLE SAM AS HE MAY APPEAR TWENTY YEARS FROM NOW

PLATE 96

PLATE 97

PLATE 98

PLATE 97
Breakfast, Round Valley, California, 1922

PLATE 98
Campers in national forest

PLATE 99
Olympic Highway, near Lake Crescent, Washington

PLATE 100
Gathering galax for floral decorations, Pisgah National Forest, North Carolina, 1913

PLATE 101
Using free timber, Black Hills National Forest, South Dakota, 1913

PLATE 102
"Bicycle tree," Snohomish, Washington, 1910

PLATE 99

PLATE 100

There are a great many interests on the National Forests which sometimes conflict a little. They must be made to fit into one another so that the machine runs smoothly as a whole. It is often necessary for one man to give a little here, another a little there. But by giving way a little at present they both profit by it a great deal in the end.

GIFFORD PINCHOT, 1907

PLATE 101

PLATE 102

43

PLATE 103

The public, now more aware of the many goods that the forest provides and that the resource may not be limitless, raised a cry for less waste and more vision. Foresters responded with increased efforts in reforestation and wood and wood product research.

PLATE 103
Yellow poplar plywood sheet, Forest Products Laboratory, 1913

PLATE 104
Planting by hand, Louisiana

PLATE 105
Planting yellow pine, Black Hills National Forest, South Dakota, 1912

PLATE 106
Nursery beds, Halsey, Nebraska, 1903

PLATE 107
Xylotomists preparing wood sections for microscopic inspection, 1911

PLATE 104

PLATE 105

PLATE 106

PLATE 107

At this hour, 2 p.m., the City of Tacoma

is practically in a state of semi-darkness, the sky

having a pinkish overcast, and the general effect is

exactly that of a reflection of a big fire at night.

There seems to be quite a little smoke of a

fog-like formation in the air, and taken all together

it is decidedly a peculiar situation.

GEORGE S. LONG, 1902

PLATE 109

PLATE 108

The late summer of 1910 approached with ominous, sinister and threatening portents. Dire catastrophe seemed to permeate the very atmosphere. Through the first weeks of August the sun arose a coppery red ball…as if announcing an impending disaster. The air felt close, oppressive and explosive, drift smoke clouded the sky day after day…. Finally the expected hurricane broke in all its fury. Local fires burned together and swept through the forest as one vast conflagration…the mid-afternoon became dark. The roar of the flames and crash of fallen timber could plainly be heard in town…

CLARENCE B. SWIM, 1910

PLATE 110

PLATE 108
Columbia National Forest, Washington, 1912

PLATE 109
Yacolt burn, Washington, 1903

PLATE 110
Newspaper headlines, August 1910

PLATE 111
Mouth of the tunnel where firefighters died, Coeur d'Alene National Forest, Idaho, 1910

PLATE 112
Burned lodgepole pine forest, Idaho, 1910

PLATE 111

PLATE 112

Got the fire under control. My knees have scabbed over and feel pretty good today, but my hands are in a hell of a shape. Damned if I'll ever fight fire with my bare hands again.

R.L. WOESNER, N.D.

PLATE 114

PLATE 113

PLATE 113
Special agent J.F. Jardine, Wallowa (now Wallowa-Whitman) National Forest, Oregon, 1908

PLATE 114
Kiosk for fire tools

PLATE 116

PLATE 115
Reporting fire by portable telephone, Crescent Mountain, Oregon

PLATE 116
Speeder fire patrol, San Joaquin and Eastern Railroad, California, 1913

PLATE 117
Rangers' wives carrying food and supplies to firefighters, 1909

PLATE 115   PLATE 117

49

1916
National Park Service is created

1916
Chamberlin-Ferris Act revests 2.8 million acres of unsold Oregon & California Railroad grant lands

1917
First issue of *Journal of Forestry* is published, combining *Forestry Quarterly* and the *Proceedings of the Society of American Foresters*

One of my pet dreams had always been of a log cabin, and here was an ideal one—indoors as cozy as could be wished, while outdoors—was a grander dooryard than any estate in the land could boast, and oh! What a prospect of glorious freedom from four walls and a time-clock.

HALLIE MORSE DAGGETT, N.D.

PLATE 119

PLATE 118

PLATE 118
Twin Sisters fire lookout, Colorado (now Arapaho-Roosevelt) National Forest, Colorado, 1917

PLATE 119
Hallie Morse Daggett, first female Forest Service fire lookout, Klamath National Forest, California (1913–1927)

PLATE 120

PLATE 121

PLATE 120
Carving propellers for fighter planes, Forest Products Laboratory, c. 1917

PLATE 121
Salvage logs for war effort

PLATE 122
10th Reserve engineers, "The Lumberjack Regiment," Washington, DC, 1917

The needs of the country for the services of men engaged in war work who have some technical training in forestry or vocational training in woodwork and the best utilization of wood are pressing, as shown in the recent call of the Army, for at least 16,000 men proficient in the inspection of wood, in lumbering, and in other vocations relating directly to the handling and utilization of forest products in the conduct of war.

WAR COMMITTEE OF THE
SOCIETY OF AMERICAN FORESTERS, 1918

PLATE 122

PLATE 123

PLATE 124

Forestry was not all about large tracts of land or growing and harvesting trees for mass consumption. Foresters were also hard at work in urban areas, offering advice on the care of city trees and engaging in such activities as tree trimming along utility lines.

PLATE 125

PLATE 126

PLATE 127

PLATE 123
Tamping seedlings into transplant beds, Monongahela National Forest, West Virginia, 1927

PLATE 124
Pulpwood mill, Bristol, Virginia, 1925

PLATE 125
Minnesota, 1935

PLATES 126 & 127
Urban tree trimming, Minnesota, 1930

After World War I, foresters set to work developing new methods and means of harvesting and regeneration. Harvesting using a selection system and the preservation of seed trees became common. In the Pacific Northwest forest industry was purchasing and managing cutover lands and establishing what would become tree farms 20 years later.

Intensive forest management was also taking place in the South, where pines and other hardwoods were steadily increasing in value. By the 1940s southern forests were supplying roughly half the nation's wood pulp.

PLATE 128

PLATE 129

PLATE 128
Clemons Logging Company tract, Washington, late 1920s

PLATE 129
Clemons Tree Farm, 1941

PLATE 130
Clemons Tree Farm, 1967

PLATE 130

PLATE 132

PLATE 133

In the 1920s and 1930s a series of natural disasters swept through the country, destroying hundreds of thousands of acres of forestland. Fires tore through much of the country, and by train, horseback, foot, and airplane firefighters arrived to battle the blaze.

PLATE 136

PLATE 137

PLATE 131
Firefighter, Pisgah National Forest, North Carolina, 1925

PLATE 132
Constructing a fireline, George Washington National Forest, Virginia, 1939

PLATE 133
Pilots, Olympic airplane patrol, Olympic National Forest, Washington, 1921

PLATE 134
Fire camp, western pine region

PLATE 135
Firefighters, Pisgah National Forest, North Carolina, 1923

PLATE 136
Saddle Mountain fire, site of 1933 Tillamook burn, Oregon, 1939

PLATE 137
Malibu fire, Angeles National Forest, California, 1935

PLATE 135

1926
Export of timber cut lawfully from national forests or public lands in Alaska is authorized

1926
First World Forestry Congress is held in Rome, Italy

1928
McNary-Woodruff Act authorizes $8 million for purchase of land under Weeks Law

1928
McSweeney-McNary Forest Research Act underwrites federal forestry research

1929
More than 100 wildlife sanctuaries are consolidated under federal protection by Norbeck-Anderson Migratory Bird Conservation Act

1930
Elm disease is detected in Holland

1930
Knutson-Vandenberg Act authorizes funding from timber receipts for reforestation of national forests

1930
First nationwide forest survey, under McSweeney-McNary Act, is initiated

1932
American Forest Products Industries is incorporated as a subsidiary of the National Lumber Manufacturers Association

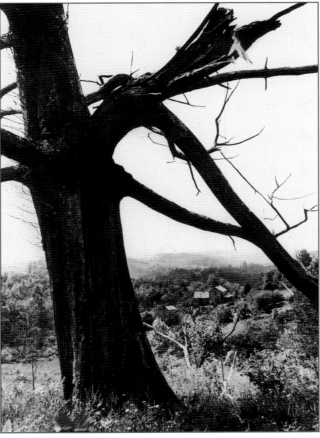

PLATE 138

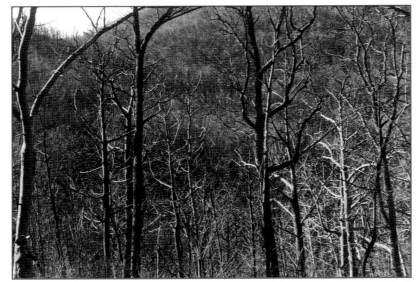

PLATE 139

Sometimes it was disease, such as chestnut blight, and infestation, such as the western pine beetle, that claimed the forest and challenged the forester. And as if that weren't enough, hurricanes roared through the Northeast, leveling forests and recreation areas and creating a plentiful supply of salvage logs. In the Midwest trees were the remedy for rather than the victims of natural devastation. From 1934 to 1943 nearly 10,000 miles of trees were planted on approximately 33,000 farms to protect farms and crops from wind and drought.

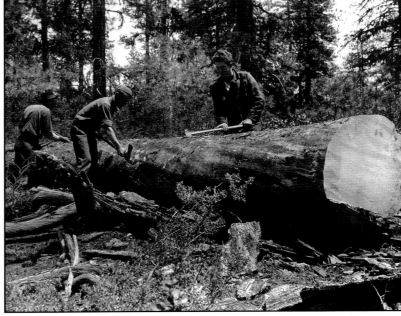

PLATE 140

PLATE 138
Dead chestnut, Virginia, 1946

PLATE 139
Blighted chestnut trees, Chattahoochee National Forest, Georgia, 1939

PLATE 140
Fell-peel-burn method of controlling western pine beetle infestation, Blacks Mountain Experimental Forest, California, 1934

PLATE 141
Harvard Forest Director Al C. Cline, overseeing salvage operations

PLATE 142 & 143
Hurricane damage, New Hampshire, winter 1938–39

PLATE 144
Raphael Zon

PLATE 145
Shelterbelt and wheatfield, Alden, Kansas, 1938

PLATE 141

Probably the social benefits from windbreaks will be as great as the physical. If, by tree planting, agriculture may be made somewhat safer in a region subject to periodic droughts; if…a diversified agriculture can be encouraged; if living conditions can be made more attractive…then the still primitive and hazardous existence in the plains region will be raised for thousands of settlers to a higher level of permanence and stability… a higher cultural life.

RAPHAEL ZON, 1935

PLATE 144

PLATE 142

PLATE 143

PLATE 145

PLATE 146

PLATE 147

I propose to create a civilian conservation corps to be used in simple work, not interfering with normal employment, and confining itself to forestry, the prevention of soil erosion, flood control and similar projects. I call your attention to the fact that this type of work is of definite, practical value, not only through the prevention of present great financial loss, but also as a means of creating future national wealth.

FRANKLIN D. ROOSEVELT, 1933

PLATE 148

PLATE 149

CCC Projects on the Bighorn National Forest

- Constructed Sibley and Meadowlark Lake dams
- Constructed Crazy Woman Canyon Road and Shell-Tensleep Road
- Constructed 80 miles of primitive fire roads
- Developed 102 acres of campgrounds
- Built 82 miles of drift fence
- Built 11 cattle guards
- Strung 88 miles of telephone line
- Constructed 25 bridges
- Planted 250,000 seedlings and thinned trees on 4,500 acres
- Fought fires for 4,148 man-days

PLATE 150

PLATE 151

PLATE 146
Franklin D. Roosevelt visiting CCC camp

PLATE 147
Superintendent Frank S. Robinson instructing workers, Lassen National Forest, California

PLATE 148
CCC camp, 1930s

PLATE 149
Trail building, Gettysburg National Park

PLATE 150
Spraying along road

PLATE 151
Building firebreak, San Bernardino National Forest, California

PLATE 152

In laboratories, nurseries, and experiment stations, researchers were working on every aspect of the structure, properties, treatment, and uses of wood. Especially significant in the 1930s was the study of the nature and effects of fire and improvements in wood as a building material.

PLATE 154

PLATE 153

PLATE 152
Fuel hygrograph, Priest River Experiment Station, Idaho, 1937

PLATE 153
Spark arrester, Virginia, 1932

PLATE 154
Fire behavior studies, Harrison Experimental Forest, Mississippi, 1937

PLATE 155

PLATE 156

PLATE 157

PLATE 155
First all-wood prefabricated house, 1937

PLATE 156
First glue-laminated arches, Forest Products Laboratory, 1935

PLATE 157
Timber test floor, Forest Products Laboratory, 1937

SMOKEY SAYS—

Care will prevent 9 out of 10 forest fires!

PLATE 158

PLATE 159

PLATE 160

PLATE 161

With the advent of World War II, the need for wood and wood products escalated dramatically. While foresters were hard at work ensuring an adequate supply of timber, loggers and mill crews were also working at capacity. But there was always a little extra time to enjoy the camaraderie and sport that went along with forestry work.

Military machines had a near-insatiable appetite for wood—pontoon bridges and railroad ties, gunstocks, ships, and docks, barracks and catonments, crates, mess halls, hospitals, post exchanges, and aircraft. Wood cellulose provided a main constitute of explosives. Glycerol made from wood produced nitroglycerine; the addition of sawdust produced dynamite. Shrapnel in warheads came packed in rosin, and turpentine fueled flamethrowers. Wood plastic formed panels and knobs for the rapidly expanding electronics field. Fighters, light bombers, and PT boats consumed mountains of especially graded Douglas-fir plywood. The single biggest use of wood was for packing crates to ship military supplies to the front. In all it required three trees to equip and maintain each American soldier.

HAROLD K. STEEN, 1970

PLATE 163

PLATE 160
Ruth Hoerschgen Turcotte (left) and June DeGraff, champion women sawyers, Roselake, Idaho

PLATE 161
Caterpillar logging, Pacific Northwest, 1937

PLATES 162, 163, 164
World War II posters supporting timber industry

PLATE 162

PLATE 164

CHAPTER THREE

PLATE 165

Conservation is a state of harmony

between man and land.

ALDO LEOPOLD, 1949

PLATE 165
Industrial tree farm,
Alabama

Get Out the Cut!

The pairing of photographs of a southern tree farm and Levittown not only reveals the postwar drive to rationalize the landscape but also suggests the crucial role forestry played in the explosive peacetime economy: rapid suburbanization was impossible without the equally speedy harvesting of timber on public and private lands. By 1950 more than 12 million acres in the South had been planted to tree farms, and there was a corresponding proliferation of mills for lumber, pulp, and paper. To meet the increasing demand for wood and its by-products, foresters made use of technological advances for "getting out the cut," and of new biological insights to accelerate trees' growth rates.

But the profession's contributions did not go uncontested. Ironically, the stiffest challenge came from middle-class suburbanites who had directly benefited from the construction of cheaper housing. Large numbers of citizens had exchanged urban decay for more bucolic settings; now they were using their rising incomes to recreate in national and state forests and parks. Their return to "nature" made them more sensitive to the claims of an emerging environmental movement—often linked to the publication of Rachel Carson's *Silent Spring*. Those who camped and hiked, hunted and fished became critical of unrestrained pesticide application and clearcutting because each damaged the wildlife and wilderness they had traveled to the Great Outdoors to enjoy.

Political pressures emanating from these developments led to the passage of such federal environmental initiatives as the Wilderness Act (1964), the National Trail System and Wild and Scenic Rivers Acts (1968), the National Environmental Policy Act (1970), the Clean Air and Water Acts (1963, 1973), and the creation of the Environmental Protection Agency (1970).

In different ways, these new legal standards established environmentalism as a central tenet of American political life, thus posing new complications for foresters. In the mid-1950s, at the height of the Cold War, they had been considered members of a much-valued scientific elite and were celebrated for their many contributions to the nation's booming economy and rising standards of living. By the early 1970s, however, following a decade of legal challenges culminating in *Izaak Walton League v. Butz* (1973), in which the Supreme Court restricted clearcutting on national forests, foresters' professional judgment was under attack and their status in doubt.

PLATE 166

The earth's vegetation is part of a web of life in which there are intimate and essential relations…Sometimes we have no choice but to disturb these relationships, but we should do so thoughtfully, with full awareness that what we do may have consequences remote in time and place.

RACHEL CARSON, 1962

PLATE 166
Levittown, New York, 1947

Association of Consulting Foresters
is established

SINCE 1948

1948

Society for Range Management is
established, spun off from SAF

1948

SAF code of ethics is adopted

PLATE 167

1949

A Sand County Almanac, by Aldo
Leopold, is published posthumously

1949

Supreme Court affirms the constitu-
tionality of state regulation of logging on private lands

1949

13 smokejumpers die at Mann
Gulch, Montana

1950

Cooperative Forest Management Act
underwrites federal and state
forestry work for private landholders

1950

1,264 tree farms in the South com-
prise 12 million acres, about half the
US total of tree farm acres

1951

The Nature Conservancy is
incorporated from a breakaway,
activist faction of the Ecological
Society of America

1952

Smokey Bear Act protects symbol
from unauthorized uses

1953

Fourth American Forest Congress
is held

PLATE 168

PLATE 169

PLATE 168
*Douglas-fir, Mount St.
Helens, Mount Adams,
and Mount Hood,
Washington*

PLATE 169
*Dave Molinaro planning
a timber sale with aerial
photos, Tongass
National Forest, Alaska,
1958*

PLATE 170
*Ranger LeRoy Sprague
using an increment
borer, Boise National
Forest, Idaho, 1955*

PLATE 171
*Forestry aide Lupe
Martinez, Carson
National Forest, New
Mexico, 1959*

PLATE 172
*Selection marking in
old-growth redwood,
Yurok Redwood
Experimental Forest,
California, 1959*

PLATE 173
*Tree marked and mea-
sured for sale, Koen
Experimental Forest,
Arkansas, 1951*

World War II generated improved aerial photography and men trained in its use and interpretation. For forestry this meant new and improved methods of conducting forest surveys. Across the country, aerial photographs were used for initial determination of acreage and forest type. Field crews then traveled to designated plots by truck and on foot to evaluate and classify stands and measure and mark trees.

PLATE 170

PLATE 171

PLATE 172

PLATE 173

PLATE 174

PLATE 175

PLATE 176

PLATE 177

PLATE 178

PLATE 179

To meet the public's need for pulp, paper, and plywood, significant harvesting of smaller-diameter trees was taking place not only in the Pacific Northwest but in the East and the South as well.

PLATE 174
Chainsaw felling of hickory, Dierks Lumber and Coal Company, Arkansas, 1948

PLATE 175
Pulpwood thinning in 50-year-old longleaf stand, Osceola National Forest, Florida, 1948

PLATE 176
Caterpillar trailing sledload of logs

PLATE 177
Plywood plant, Longview, Washington, 1947

PLATE 178
Wood veneer, Forest Products Laboratory

PLATE 179
Paper mill, Georgetown, South Carolina, c. 1946

PLATE 180
Carload of pulp logs for a Masonite plant, Jones County, Mississippi, 1948

PLATE 180

PLATE 182

PLATE 183

Commemorating
FIFTH WORLD FORESTRY CONGRESS

SEATTLE, WASHINGTON
August 29 to September 10, 1960

PLATE 181

PLATE 185

PLATE 184

The regeneration of harvested areas was a concern for both private landowners and public agencies. Large and small tree farms, supported by nurseries and research facilities, were rapidly being established to ensure future generations of trees.

PLATE 187

PLATE 186

PLATE 182
Weeding at Forest Industries tree farm, Washington

PLATE 183
Sorting and culling slash pine seedlings, DeSoto National Forest, Mississippi, 1951

PLATE 184
Clearcut, Mount St. Helens tree farm, Washington

PLATE 185
Master Forest Farmer Hein Temple, Tioga County, New York, 1948

PLATE 186
Kenneth B. Pomeroy studying soil conditions for loblolly pine, Duke University, Durham, North Carolina

PLATE 187
Using larvicide, or tear gas, to sterilize soil, Snoqualmie Falls Lumber Company tree nursery, Washington, 1940s

PLATE 188
Planting pine seedlings, Yazoo–Lake Tallahatchie Flood Prevention Project, near Oxford, Mississippi, 1954

PLATE 188

Forests and foresters play an important role in ensuring water quality and protecting watersheds. In the 1950s, many local farmers participated in the Yazoo–Lake Tallahatchie Flood Prevention Project in Mississippi. By planting loblolly pine trees, they were able to stop erosion in former cotton fields.

1961
Silent Spring, by Rachel Carson, is published

1962
Outdoor Recreation Review Commission report stresses importance of outdoor recreation

1962
McIntire-Stennis Forestry Research Act funds forestry research in universities and land-grant institutions

1963
Clean Air Act is passed

1963
Fifth American Forest Congress is held in Washington, DC

1964
Wilderness Act is passed, creating National Wilderness Preservation System

1964
Land and Water Conservation Fund establishes funding for federal land acquisition and for state recreation programs

1966
Endangered Species Preservation Act is passed

1966
National Wildlife Refuge System Administration Act consolidates refuges and protected land into one system

1967
Environmental Defense Fund is formed

PLATE 189

The Secretary of Agriculture is authorized and directed to develop and administer the renewable surface resources of the national forests for multiple use and sustained yield of the several products and services obtained therefrom.

MULTIPLE USE SUSTAINED YIELD ACT OF 1960

PLATE 190

PLATE 190
Hikers, Mount Rainier, Washington, 1958

PLATE 191
Howard Zahnhiser

PLATE 192
Campers, George Washington National Forest, Virginia, 1968

PLATES 193 & 194
St. Paul, Minnesota, 1970s

We deeply need the humility to know ourselves as the dependent members of a great community of life, and this can indeed be one of the spiritual benefits of a wilderness experience.

HOWARD ZAHNHISER, 1955

PLATE 191

PLATE 193

PLATE 192

By the mid-1970s millions of urban shade trees had been destroyed by Dutch elm disease; over a two-year period, 50,000 trees were lost in Minneapolis alone. In a remarkable recovery effort, urban foresters convinced Minnesota legislators to allocate state monies for municipal street care. As a result nearly half of the 200,000 elm trees in Minneapolis were saved; more than 150,000 trees have been planted to replace those lost to the disease. Shown here is a street in St. Paul before and after removal of diseased trees.

PLATE 194

| 1969 | Endangered Species Conservation Act creates list of threatened species |

PLATE 195

| 1969 | Friends of the Earth is organized |

| 1970 | National Environmental Policy Act (NEPA) establishes Council on Environmental Quality |

| 1970 | Environmental Protection Agency is created |

| 1970 | Denis Hayes organizes Earth Day |

High Yield Forestry…it's a way of managing our forests that will produce more than twice the volume of wood that Mother Nature could alone.

WEYERHAEUSER ADVERTISEMENT

| 1970 | Natural Resources Defense Council is created |

| 1971 | Roadless Area Review and Evaluation (RARE) is initiated |

| 1972 | Clean Water Act passes Congress |

| 1972 | RARE I is halted after district court ruling that exclusions of some areas violated NEPA |

| 1972 | Renewable Natural Resources Foundation is formed |

PLATE 197

PLATE 198

| 1973 | In *Izaak Walton League v. Butz* a district court rules that clearcutting on Monongahela National Forest violates provisions of 1897 Organic Act |

| 1973 | Endangered Species Act provides legal protection for species and their ecosystems |

PLATE 196

PLATE 197
Illo Gauditz injecting extract of Douglas-fir tissue into gas chromatograph, Centralia, Washington, 1965

PLATE 198
James Dick demonstrating encapsulated seedling gun, Washington, 1967

PLATE 199

PLATE 200

Intensive forest management, made possible by advances in biological and chemical research, took hold in the 1960s. Seeds, gleaned from hand-gathered cones, were germinated in laboratories and then transplanted to nursery beds. Seedlings were transplanted, fertilized, grafted, and thinned according to careful calculations. Final harvest occurred at around age 45, and then the cycle began again.

PLATE 201

PLATE 202

...the public's demand for wood for housing and for paper products will be met because trees can be grown, harvested and manufactured cheaply and efficiently....The role of clearcutting in forest management can be fully understood only if the harvest of a mature forest by this system is recognized as the beginning of a new and more efficiently managed forest.

GEORGE R. STAEBLER, 1971

PLATE 203

The post-war production boom may have justified the single-minded emphasis on timber production. But the continued emphasis largely ignores the economics of regeneration; it ignores related forest values; it ignores local social concerns; and it is simply out of step with changes in our society since the post-war years...

ARNOLD BOLLE, 1970

PLATE 203
Terraces on Bitterroot National Forest, Montana

We hope to involve an entire society in a rethinking of many of its basic assumptions.

PLATE 204

Earth Day will have to be extended to Earth Year, Decade, Generation if the poisoning of water, air, and soil is to be halted or even appreciably slowed down.

PLATE 205

The environment is where we all meet; where we all have a mutual interest; it is one thing that all of us share. Whatever its condition, it is, after all, a reflection of ourselves—our tastes, our aspirations, our successes, and our failures.

LADY BIRD JOHNSON, 1988

PLATE 205
The Quincy Library Group, Quincy, California, 1998

NEW VISIONS

The desire to strike a more harmonious balance between the environment and humanity—to which Lady Bird Johnson and William Cronon have lent their considerable eloquence—has been especially poignant at the close of the twentieth century. At no time has public discussion of environmental matters been more discordant.

Professional foresters have been in the thick of this debate over the management and use of natural resources in the United States. New federal regulations have required innovative management strategies, the articulation of which has been frequently challenged in the courts, legislatures, and media. Added to this divisiveness has been the intensifying competition between resource and recreational users of mountain, forest, and stream, and the rapid outward thrust of urban areas into wildlands. An apt marker of the cultural tensions that foresters must mediate is this curious paradox: Americans' growing, almost mystical appreciation of Ancient Forests comes conjoined with their hunger to consume, through the purchase of wood products, these emblems of unspoiled nature.

Navigating these aesthetic and political conundrums has been treacherous. But to focus solely on the complications is to miss equally important developments in professional practice. Space-race engineering produced new techniques that have enabled foresters to better visualize and understand the land's physical contours and biological complexities. Other research has altered firefighting protocols: once rigorously suppressed, managed fire is now recognized as critical to the maintenance of healthy forests and the protection of residential and recreational areas. Transformative, too, have been biotechnological innovations that accelerate the growth of select tree species, which when combined with advances in material conservation and composition, have expanded lumber reserves while meeting the needs of a growing population.

Those changes, along with the bruising battles over Pacific Northwest timber harvests in the late 1980s, altered the context for discussions of the protection of endangered species and threatened economies. The 1993 Forest Conference in Portland, Oregon, represented an early attempt to establish common ground between environmental activists, industry representatives, and lumber communities, as did the local partnership known as the Quincy (California) Library Group (1992) and the Seventh American Forest Congress (1996). From these collaborative experiences has emerged broad agreement that the sustainability of ecosystems, markets, and societies is now the foundation of good forest management.

Sustainable forestry will not resolve all future disputes, but that is to be expected in a culture that has so defined itself through its evolving relationship to the land. The significance of this for foresters? The profession's second century will be as confounding and compelling as the first.

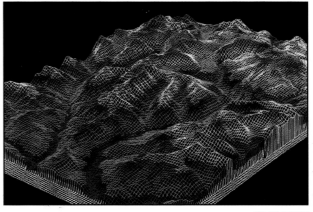

PLATE 206

Nature is all we've got: we are never outside of it, and our lives depend on it.

WILLIAM CRONON, 1999

PLATE 206
Perspective view of elevation model, Gifford Pinchot National Forest

PLATE 207

PLATE 208

PLATE 209

In response to public scrutiny and government regulations, the forestry community intensified efforts to perfect low-impact harvesting methods. The methods developed in the early 1970s were certainly innovative, although not all of them turned out to be practical. Helicopter logging, however, continues to be a viable method of harvesting in areas where roads are potentially damaging or impossible due to the terrain.

PLATE 207
"Sky Hook," early 1970s

PLATE 208
Artist rendering of the Piasecki Heli-Stat, early 1970s

PLATE 209
Helicopter skidding, Plumas National Forest, California, early 1970s

PLATE 210
Balloon logging, early 1970s

PLATE 210

New on-the-ground machinery was also important in addressing environmental and economic concerns. To supply the nation's ever-increasing need for pulpwood, the harvesting of small-diameter trees was becoming common, especially in the South. Equipment such as the field chipper and whole tree harvester were well suited for such operations and limited damage to surrounding trees and soil.

PLATE 211

PLATE 212

PLATE 211
Southern pine plantation near Birmingham, Alabama, 1986

PLATE 212
Poles, southeastern United States, 1998

PLATE 213

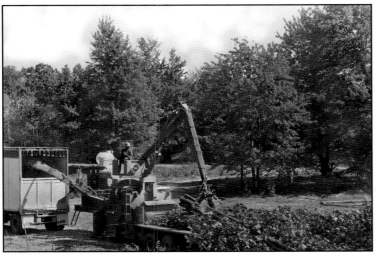

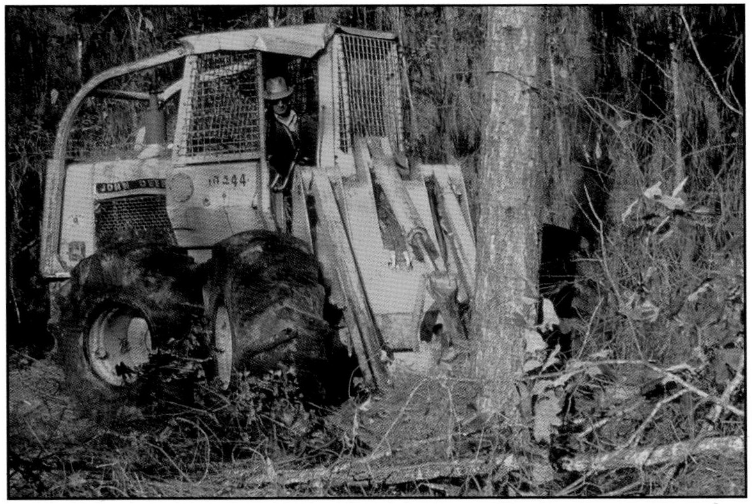

PLATE 214

PLATE 216

PLATE 215

PLATE 213
Field chipper, early 1970s

PLATE 214
"Feller buncher" cuts trees automatically

PLATE 215
Moving pine logs, Georgia, 1992

PLATE 216
Whole tree harvester

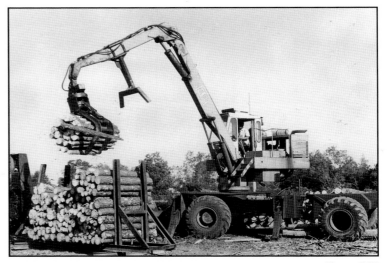

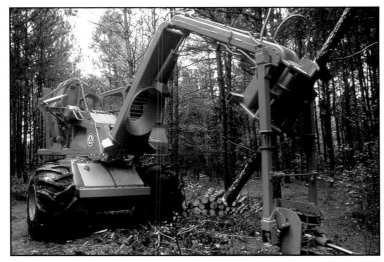

Product research and development progressed apace with new harvesting methods and equipment and public demands for less waste. The Forest Products Laboratory developed a variety of means to maximize yield through improved milling and manufacturing operations. The lab also combined wood with other materials, such as plastics; created products that use waste and more recycled material; and developed a biopulping process, which increases efficiency and reduces environmental impact.

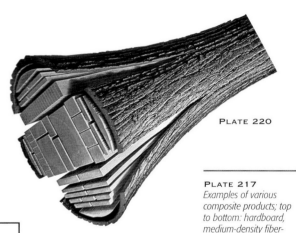

PLATE 218

PLATE 217

PLATE 221

The Truss Frame System, in which roof, wall, and floor trusses are manufactured and assembled offsite, expedites home building and enhances durability in areas where high winds are a problem.

PLATE 219

PLATE 220

PLATE 217
Examples of various composite products; top to bottom: hardboard, medium-density fiberboard, particleboard, oriented-strand board, plywood

PLATE 218
Overview of 50-ton outdoor biopulping site, 1999

PLATE 219
Cement-bonded panel

PLATE 220
Best Open Face system maximizes yield from logs for automated mill systems, 1971

PLATE 221
Truss-framed construction, 1982

PLATE 222

PLATE 223

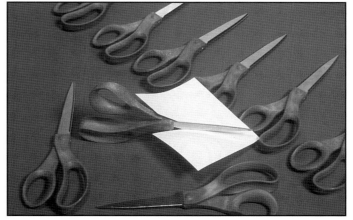

PLATE 224

The average American uses the equivalent of a 100-foot high tree, 16 inches in diameter, each year for wood and paper needs. About 45 percent of the paper consumed in the United States is recovered for recycling.

AMERICAN FOREST AND
PAPER ASSOCIATION, 1995

PLATE 222
Space board, made from
water and recycled fiber

PLATE 223
Recycled material used in
car door panels

PLATE 224
Injection-molded scissor
handles made from
wood flour and plastic
feedstock

PLATE 225
"Recycled house"
demonstrates that 20%
of materials in housing
can be manufactured
from recycled wastes

PLATE 225

PLATE 226

With the launch of the Landsat-1 in 1972, foresters gained a new way of seeing the forest and the trees. Contemporary remote sensing and geographic information systems technology enable foresters to use data gathered via satellite to plan harvesting and regeneration activities, enhance biological diversity, and monitor fire and atmospheric conditions.

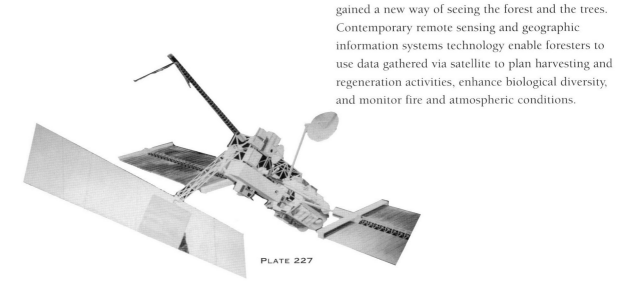

PLATE 227

PLATE 228

PLATE 229

PLATE 230

PLATE 226
*Computerized digitizer,
1970s*

PLATE 227
Landsat satellite

PLATE 228
*Using GPS for data
collection*

PLATE 229
*Using GPS equipment
in the field*

PLATE 230
*Using GPS to map fire
area, Oakland Hills,
California, 1992*

PLATE 231

PLATE 233

PLATE 234

PLATE 232

PLATE 231
John Woods uses GIS to monitor bear migration zones in Swan Valley, Montana

PLATE 232
GIS map of potential natural vegetation, Gifford Pinchot National Forest, Washington

PLATES 233 & 234
Images derived from forest inventory data, Queen Charlotte Island, British Columbia

Geographic imaging and specialized desktop software allow foresters to generate multiple landscape views based on various harvesting and regeneration scenarios. This can be especially useful in discussing management plans with citizen groups.

PLATE 236

PLATE 235

PLATE 237

On May 18, 1980, Washington State was rocked by the eruption of Mount St. Helens. Some 150,000 acres of private, state, and federal land was destroyed that day along with the idyllic Spirit Lake. The management objective in congressionally designated Monument lands is to allow nature to take its course; reforestation on private land began in 1981.

PLATE 239

PLATE 238

Fires continue to be a major feature of forested areas. When those areas are also the transient home for thousands of tourists, the fires can be particularly dangerous and recovery a very public endeavor. In 1988, fires burned some 995,000 acres in Yellowstone National Park. During the 10 years that followed, the vegetation and wildlife returned, as did the tourists.

PLATE 240

PLATE 241

PLATES 240 & 241
Yellowstone National Park, Wyoming, 1988

PLATE 242

PLATE 243

PLATE 244

PLATES 242,
243, 244
*Yellowstone National
Park, Wyoming, 1992*

PLATE 245
*Yellowstone National
Park, 1998*

PLATE 245

PLATE 246

PLATE 247

PLATE 248

PLATE 246
*Rabbit Fire, Idaho City
complex, 1994*

PLATE 247
*Firefighters, Foothills Fire,
Idaho, 1992*

PLATE 248
*Firefighter, County Line
Fire, Idaho, 1992*

Each year thousands of men and women join fire teams to battle blazes across the country. Experiments are currently being conducted to improve fire-control procedures and the personal shelters designed to protect workers from the red-hot heat and smoke of a burning forest. The shelters shown here are made of aluminum foil and glass; they weigh three pounds and fold up neatly into a pouch carried on the firefighter's belt. Inside the shelter, the temperature can rise to 200 degrees.

PLATE 250

PLATE 249

PLATE 249
Testing fire shelter performance under crown fire conditions, Northwest Territories, 1999

PLATE 250
Personal fire shelter

Where the forest meets the city, fire is especially problematic and fire-fighting challenging. Wildfires can rapidly encroach on residential areas, putting homes and citizens at risk. In some cases, prescribed fire is the best approach to limit fuel load and minimize risk. Communities are also debating how to restrict sprawl and thus lower fire danger.

PLATE 252

PLATE 251

PLATE 253

PLATE 251
Water drop, County Line fire, Idaho, 1992

PLATE 252
Chemical retardant drop, Rabbit Fire, Sunset Lookout, Idaho, 1994

PLATE 253
Prescribed burn, Cottonwood, Idaho, 1994

PLATE 254

...too hot, destructive, dangerous, and too ecologically, economically, aesthetically, and socially damaging to be tolerable...We cannot, in my opinion, simply step back and wait for nature to take its course.

JACK WARD THOMAS, 1994

PLATE 255

PLATE 254
*8th Street fire,
Crane Creek golf
course, Idaho, 1996*

PLATE 255
*Los Angeles County,
California*

PLATE 256

PLATE 257

If wildness can stop being (just) out there and start

being (also) in here, if it can start being as humane

as it is natural, then perhaps we can get on with the

unending task of struggling to live rightly in the

world—not just in the garden, not just in wilderness,

but in the home that encompasses them both.

WILLIAM CRONON, 1996

PLATE 256
Winnipeg, Manitoba

PLATE 257
*Looking toward
Frank Church River of
No Return Wilderness
from outside Stanley,
Idaho, 1992*

As more and more Americans live in urban areas, more and more foresters are specializing in urban and community forestry. They work with city planners and utility companies, and help residents plant and manage street trees and natural areas. Urban forests not only provide aesthetic and environmental benefits but also make it possible for all citizens to have access to trees and forest ecosystems.

PLATE 258

PLATE 259

PLATE 260

PLATE 258
Right-of-way utility trimming, central Minnesota, 1980s

PLATE 259
John Pogue plants live oak with 90-inch tree spade, Huntsville, Texas, 1999

PLATE 260
Stanley Park, Vancouver, British Columbia, 1992

1983
Forest Service identifies northern spotted owl as "indicator species" for health of old-growth forest habitats

1985
SAF sponsors "Women in Natural Resources: Challenges and Strategies" symposium in Dallas

1987
The World Commission on Environment and Development issues *Our Common Future*, an early call for sustainable global development

1987
Congress passes Timber Bridge Initiative to encourage use of wood as a structural material for highway bridges

1987
GreenWood petitions Fish and Wildlife Service to list northern spotted owl under the Endangered Species Act; environmental coalition challenges 200 BLM timber sales in court; Fish and Wildlife Service is sued for denying owl petition

1988
Ninth Circuit Court of Appeals issues emergency injunction against BLM timber sales; District court finds Fish and Wildlife decision not to list spotted owl "arbitrary and capricious"

1989
Association of Forest Service Employees for Environmental Ethics is organized

1989
Environmentalists sue Forest Service, challenging spotted owl management plan for violating NFMA, NEPA, and Migratory Bird Treaty Act (but not ESA)

In the 1980s the northern spotted owl was the focal point of a battle between environmental activists, the logging community, and elements of the forestry profession. The groups proclaimed their positions in a variety of venues, from the forest to the state house and from the editorial page to the roadways.

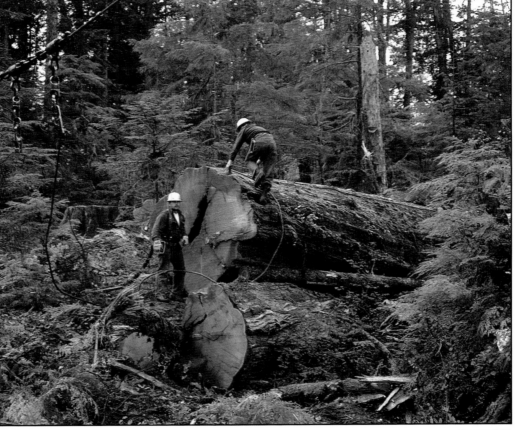

PLATE 261

PLATE 261
Harvesting old-growth western redcedar, Quinault Indian Reservation, Washington, 1982

PLATE 262
Northern spotted owl

PLATE 263
Logger

PLATE 262

PLATE 263

The debate centers on how all public forest lands
should be managed to recognize the need to protect
and preserve old-growth forests, fish, wildlife, and
water as well as the needs of the workers, businesses,
and communities dependent on timber sales.

WILLIAM J. CLINTON, 1993

1990

Rainforest Alliance announces SmartWood program to provide independent certification of environmental attributes of wood products

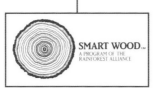

1990

Tongass Timber Reform Act repeals the funding guarantee for Forest Service timber sales in Alaska

1990

Fish and Wildlife Service lists spotted owl as threatened; Interagency Scientific Committee issues recommendations for spotted owl management

1990

National Indian Forest Resources Management Act directs secretary of Interior to obtain independent assessment of status of Indian forest resources and management

1991

Minority Participation in Forestry and Related Renewable Natural Resources, or MINFORS, holds first conference

1991

Secretary of Interior convenes an Endangered Species Committee to review Fish and Wildlife Service jeopardy opinion on BLM timber sales; in 1992 committee overrules opinion on a portion of sales but issues restrictive recommendations for preventing recurrence of this problem

PLATE 264

Let us continue to do what we have done, which is grow trees better than anybody else in the world, so that we can have not only healthy forests in the future but a healthy economy too.

NADINE BAILEY, 1993

We must disturb no more of the last remaining centers of biodiversity. These are the refuges and the seed sources for tomorrow's forests, tomorrow's wildlife, and tomorrow's economy.

JULIE NORMAN, 1993

PLATE 265

PLATE 264
*Chehalis, Washington,
June 1989*

PLATE 265
*Blue River Ranger Station,
Willamette National
Forest, Oregon, 1990*

PLATE 266

PLATE 267

PLATE 266
*Blue River Ranger Station,
Willamette National
Forest, Oregon, 1990*

PLATE 267
*Sylvester Park, Olympia,
Washington, June 1991*

*The greatest challenge that foresters and other
natural resource management professionals face in
the practice of their professions may not be the
technical aspects of forest management, but public
acceptance of those practices.*

JACK WARD THOMAS, 1997

PLATE 268

1992
Society of American Foresters adds
land ethic canon to Code of Ethics

1992
Earth Summit in Rio de Janeiro
produces international agreements
on global environmental matters

1992
Forest Service and other federal
agencies announce ecosystem
management as the approach to
implementing their missions

1993
Congress passes Urban and
Community Forestry Assistance Act,
expanding federal funding for
urban forestry

1993
President Clinton's Pacific Northwest
Forest Summit, held in Portland,
Oregon, leads to FEMAT Assessment
and President's Plan for the Pacific
Northwest Forests, which allows
courts to lift spotted owl injunction

1993
National Forest Products Association,
American Forest Council, and
American Paper Institute merge,
forming the American Forest and
Paper Association

AF&PA®

Ecosystem management requires us to reject a utilitarian view of nature and management practices judged mainly by the criterion of economic efficiency, and instead adopt an experimental, adaptive approach to resource management based on an exploration of ecological principles.

HANNAH CORTNER AND MARGARET MOOTE, 1999

PLATE 269

PLATE 268
Tagging a juvenile spotted owl, Quinault Indian Reservation, Washington, 1996

PLATE 269
Ennis timber sale, Willamette National Forest, Oregon; old and new snags left for wildlife habitat, 1990

Logical evolution, paradigm shift, or disaster in the making? Statements representing all views were voiced in the 1990s following adoption, by some government agencies and private corporations, of ecosystem management—a strategy of forest management for environmental, economic, and social benefits. Managing forestland for wildlife habitat and biodiversity as well as timber production is a major component of this management approach.

PLATE 270

There are two words that…I have learned to avoid when I explain resource programs to many groups: "ecosystem" (the e-word) and "sustainability." What these terms mean to many is "limitation" and "regulation."

J. CRAIG WHITTEKIEND, 1999

PLATE 270
Red-cockaded woodpecker habitat, Orangeburg County, South Carolina, 1998

103

Wild species are to be treasured as sources of genetic material evolved over thousands or millions of years in ways exactly tuned to individual habitats.

E.O. WILSON, 1991

PLATE 271

PLATE 272

PLATE 271
Eastern collared lizard, Missouri, 1997

PLATE 272
Ethel Hickey with federally endangered running buffalo clover, Missouri, 1993

PLATE 274

Forest ecosystems are, obviously, greatly influenced by water. But forests also play an important role in the availability and quality of water. One of their most important functions is the creation of litter and woody debris. This material, which decays to form the forest floor, increases the water-holding capacity of the soil and works as a natural filtration system. Large woody debris from the forest provides habitat for many water-dwelling creatures.

PLATE 273

PLATE 273
Comparing effectiveness of large woody debris logs and an engineered substitute to create pools and cover for fish habitat restoration, Griffin Creek, Washington, 1999

PLATE 274
Jumping salmon

PLATE 275
Roaring Creek, Greenbriar County, West Virginia, 1998

PLATE 276
Lorri Woods establishes buffer zone near stream, Columbia Falls, Montana

PLATE 276   PLATE 275

PLATE 277

PLATE 278

PLATE 279

PLATE 280

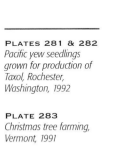

PLATE 282

In response to public pressure and legislative restrictions on timber harvests, logging communities developed alternative forest-related industries, from mushroom harvesting to Christmas tree farming. Private industry also focused on new technology and wood products, such as Taxol, used to treat some forms of cancer. Recreation continues to be a major activity on both private and public forestlands and is incorporated into management plans and strategic objectives.

PLATE 281

PLATES 281 & 282
Pacific yew seedlings grown for production of Taxol, Rochester, Washington, 1992

PLATE 283
Christmas tree farming, Vermont, 1991

PLATE 284
Tom Love carrying chanterelle mushrooms, Olympic Peninsula, Washington, 1995

PLATE 285
Harvesting morel mushrooms in year following a forest fire, Tok, Alaska

PLATE 283

PLATE 284

PLATE 285

As the population grows and public demand for multiple forest benefits increases, forestry research has focused on genetic tree improvement and clonal forestry, especially in the South. By planting fast-growing species, such as cottonwood and sweetgum, forestland owners can produce large quantities of timber resources, thus allowing other forest-lands to provide other benefits.

PLATE 286

PLATE 287

PLATE 290

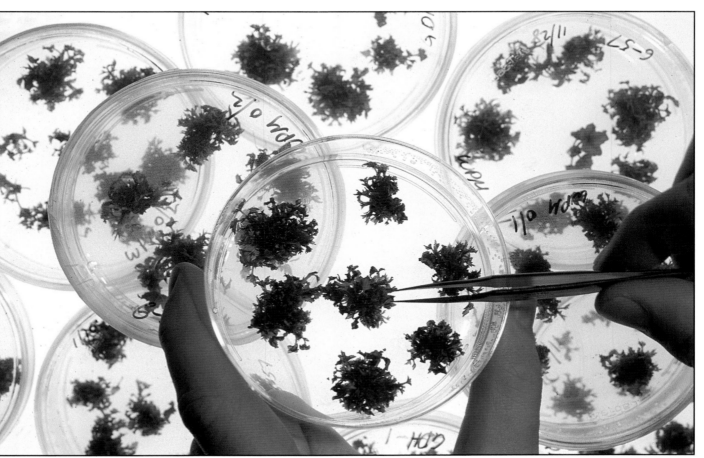

PLATE 289

PLATE 288

PLATE 286
Monitoring genetically engineered seedlings

PLATE 287
First field planting (at one year) of genetically engineered tree species (clonal sweetgum) by a forest products company

PLATE 288
Cloning loblolly pine

PLATE 289
Applying gibberellic acid to loblolly pine shoot to stimulate early flowering

PLATE 290
Measuring seed cones

PLATE 291

PLATE 291
Checking the root struc-
ture and other aspects to
determine planting time

PLATE 292
Four-year-old clonal
cottonwood, Georgia

Biotechnology will do for forest productivity what Einstein did for physics. We'll not only see opportunities to change fiber and wood properties to increase manufacturing efficiency and improve wood-based products, but we'll see large increases in the productivity of managed forests, which will reduce the pressure on natural forests worldwide.

JIM RAKESTRAW, 1999

PLATE 292

Although forestry has long had a political component, discussion about the out of doors figuratively and literally has moved indoors as foresters and legislators work on state and federal policy regarding species and land management. Elected officials are becoming well versed on forestry issues, and foresters adept at working with them in their professional practice.

PLATE 293

PLATE 294

PLATE 295

PLATE 293
Senator Larry Craig (R-ID), chair, Senate Subcommittee on Forests and Public Lands

PLATE 294
William H. Banzhaf (r), Society of American Foresters, and Don Amador, Blue Ribbon Coalition, testify before House Subcommittee on Forests and Forest Health, 1998

PLATE 295
r to l: Oregon Governor John Kitzhaber, USDA Forest Service Chief Mike Dombeck, USDA Undersecretary for Natural Resources and the Environment James Lyons, and Oregon citizens, 1999

At the same time, foresters and community activists are joining forces to find new ways of sharing their disparate experiences and perspectives. One example is the Seventh American Forest Congress, which brought together 1,500 individuals for four days in 1996.

PLATE 296

PLATE 297

PLATE 298

The whole idea here is that this is a citizens' conference; it is not a bunch of experts getting together to say, "OK, this is how we are going to run the country's forests."

JOHN GORDON, 1995

PLATES 296, 297, 298
Seventh American Forest Congress, Washington, DC, February 1996

1994

Forest Stewardship Council announces principles and criteria for sustainable forest management

1994

American Forest and Paper Association announces Sustainable Forestry Initiative

1995

The Santiago Declaration on the Conservation and Sustainable Management of Temperate and Boreal Forests is signed by the United States and nine other nations

PLATE 299

1995

Emergency Salvage Timber Sale Program ("the Timber Salvage Rider") is enacted

1996

Seventh American Forest Congress is held in Washington, DC

1999

Forest of Discord is published by the Society of American Foresters

1999

Bald eagle is recommended for removal from endangered species list

PLATE 300

Following the United Nations Conference on Environment and Development, held in Rio de Janeiro, Brazil, in 1992, the United States announced its commitment to achieving sustainable forest management by 2000. Seven criteria, along with specific indicators, were developed to help characterize and measure success. Private industry and public agencies have developed programs to develop and monitor management practices. Independent groups are often engaged to evaluate and certify landowner practices and forest products.

PLATE 301

PLATE 302

If the community takes care of the forest, the forest will take care of the community.

LYNN JUNGWIRTH, 1996

PLATE 304

PLATE 303

Criteria for the Conservation and Sustainable Management of Temperate and Boreal Forests

- Conservation of biological diversity
- Maintenance of productive capacity of forest ecosystems
- Maintenance of forest ecosystem health and vitality
- Conservation and maintenance of soil and water resources
- Maintenance of forest contribution to global carbon cycles
- Maintenance and enhancement of long-term multiple socioeconomic benefits to meet the needs of societies
- Legal, institutional, and economic framework for forest conservation and sustainable management

THE SANTIAGO DECLARATION, 1995

PLATE 305

PLATE 306

Perhaps the way to the future is not a path, but a stream—meandering and dividing, braiding and converging, flowing relentlessly toward the future. We are all part of the stream, each making our own contributions.

JANE DIFLEY, 1993

Working with nonindustrial forest landowners is one of the most exciting frontiers in our future. With proper professional guidance, some of the best forest management will be conducted on these lands, as they are far more than just an investment to their owners, but are an intensely personal interest.

MICHAEL WEBB, 1996

PLATE 305
Roaring Creek, Green Briar County, West Virginia, 1998

PLATE 306
Allegheny National Forest, Pennsylvania

PLATE 307

PLATE 308

*If 20th-century forestry was about simplifying systems,
producing wood, and managing at the stand level,
21st-century forestry will be defined by understanding
and managing complexity, providing a wide range of
ecological goods and services, and managing across
broad landscapes.*

KATHRYN KOHM AND JERRY FRANKLIN, 1997

*Where do we go from here?…we unite as family and
we begin to do the work that lets us leave behind a
legacy of love for our natural resources to be enjoyed
in perpetuity by all humans yet to walk this earth.*

TED STRONG, 1993

PLATE 309